WHAT'S INSIDE A VCR?

ARNOLD RINGSTAD

![The Child's World logo]
The Child's World®
childsworld.com

Published by The Child's World®
1980 Lookout Drive • Mankato, MN 56003-1705
800-599-READ • www.childsworld.com

Photographs ©: Rick Orndorf, cover (VCR), 1 (VCR), 4, 7, 9, 11, 15, 17 (top), 17 (bottom), 19 (top), 19 (bottom), 24; Shutterstock Images, cover (cassette), cover (motor), 1 (cassette), 1 (motor), 2, 3 (circuit board), 3 (plug), 5 (glasses), 6 (cassette), 8 (screw), 10 (cassette), 10 (screw), 12, 13, 14, 16 (bulb), 16 (cord), 18, 20, 21 (bulb), 21 (screw), 23; Praiwun Thungsarn/Shutterstock Images, 3 (screwdriver), 5 (screwdriver), 8 (screwdriver), 22; Shyripa Alexandr/Shutterstock Images, 5 (gloves)

ISBN 9781503832107
LCCN 2018962816

Printed in the United States of America
PA02419

About the Author

Arnold Ringstad lives in Minnesota.

He watched movies on a VCR when he was a kid.

Contents

Materials and Safety

Materials

☐ Safety glasses
☐ Screwdriver
☐ VCR
☐ Work gloves

Safety

• Unplug the VCR, then cut the power cord before taking it apart. Throw the end of the power cord away.

• Be careful when handling sharp objects, such as screwdrivers.

VCR

• Wear work gloves to protect your hands from sharp edges.

• Wear safety glasses in case pieces snap off.

Work gloves

Screwdriver

Safety glasses

Inside a VCR

In the 1970s, people could not watch videos online. They also did not have DVDs. A new invention in 1976 changed everything. It was called the VCR. This machine let people watch video **cassettes**. They could even record TV shows to watch them later. How does a VCR work? What's inside?

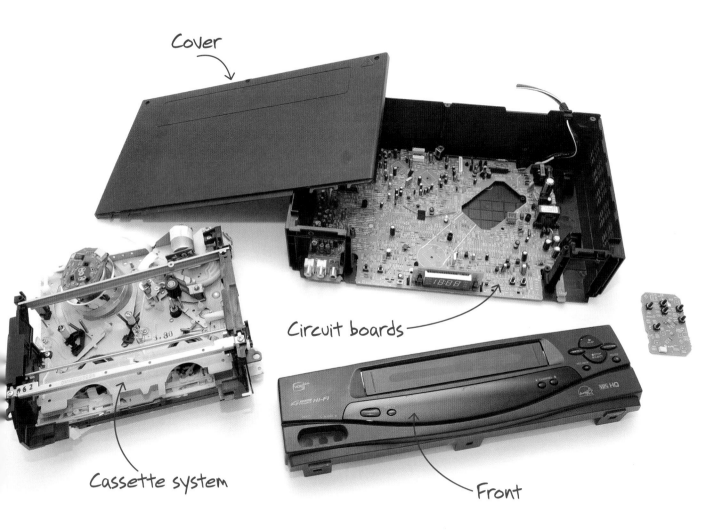

Cover

Circuit boards

Cassette system

Front

Opening the VCR

There are screws on the cover of the VCR. Use a screwdriver to remove them. Then you can pull the cover away. Plastic tabs hold the front in place. Pull on the tabs to remove the front. Now you can see the inside of the VCR.

Safety Note
Unplug the VCR, then cut the power cord before taking it apart.

The Cassette System

Inside the VCR is a frame made of metal and plastic. A few screws hold it in place. Remove them, and you can pull out the frame. This is the cassette system. It has a drum, **motors**, gears, and rollers.

Safety Note

The cassette system may have sharp edges. Be careful when removing it.

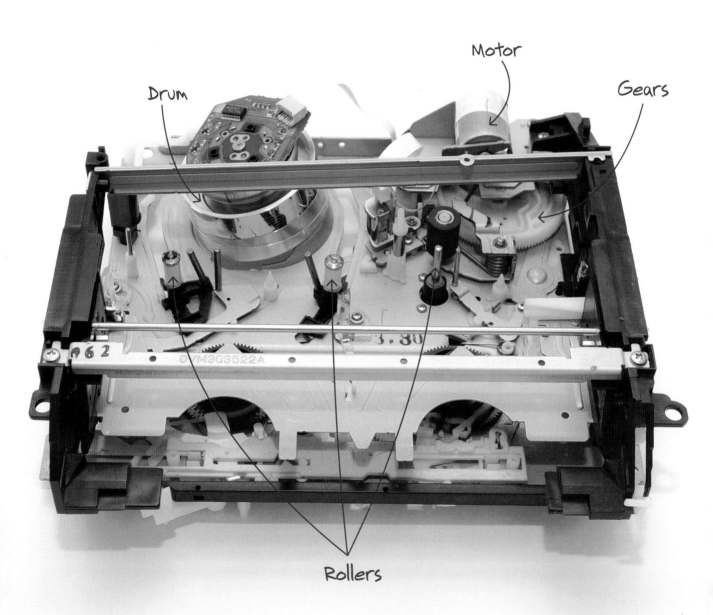

Motor

Drum

Gears

Rollers

VHS Cassettes

The cassettes that go in a VCR are called VHS cassettes. They are made of a type of hard plastic.

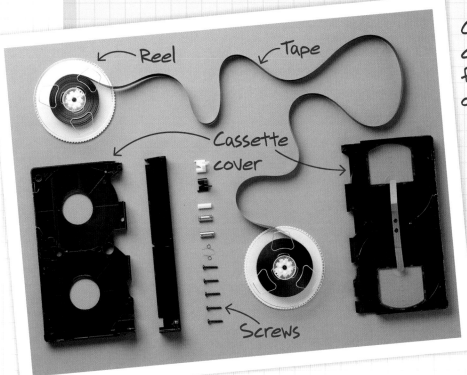

Reel

Tape

Cassette cover

Screws

Cassettes contain a long, flexible piece of plastic.

Inside are two reels. The tape winds around them. The tape is a thin sheet of flexible plastic. It is magnetic. That means a magnet can store audio and video signals on the tape. The VCR reads these signals and sends them to a TV. The TV turns them into a picture and sound.

Tape

The Drum and the Heads

When a person puts a cassette in the VCR, the top of the cassette opens up. The VCR's rollers pull the tape out. They wrap the tape around the drum. A motor makes this piece of metal spin rapidly. It contains four parts called heads.

Drum

Head

The heads are small magnets.
They read the video signals from
the magnetic tape.

The Circuit Board

Below the cassette system is a large **circuit board**. The circuit board has many jobs. It receives signals from the heads. Then it sends these signals to audio and video **jacks**. The jacks carry the signals to a TV. The circuit board takes in electricity from the power cord. This provides the energy the VCR needs to work.

Audio and video jacks

Power cord

Audio and video jacks

Circuit board

Switches and Display

The VCR has two small circuit boards. One has the display. It shows the time. Another circuit board has switches. Buttons in the front press these switches. They tell the VCR to play, pause, or stop.

Safety Note

The circuit boards may have exposed sharp parts. Be sure to wear gloves when handling them.

The display shows what time it is.

A small circuit board has switches on it.

Reusing a VCR

We've taken apart a VCR and learned what's inside. Now what? Here are some ideas for how to reuse the parts of a VCR. Can you think of any more?

- **VCR Mailbox:** Remove the parts inside of the VCR, then put the front and cover back on. Slide in letters or notes through the tape slot!

- **Follow the Gears:** The underside of the cassette system has a complicated set of gears. Try turning them with your finger. How many other gears turn? Trace where the motion goes.

Glossary

cassettes (ka-SETS): Cassettes are plastic containers that hold video tape. Videos that go into the VCR are called VHS cassettes.

circuit board (SUR-kit BORD): A circuit board is a piece of material that holds computer chips, switches, and other parts. Inside the VCR, the circuit board receives signals from the drum and sends them to the jacks.

jacks (JAX): Jacks are places where cords can plug in to send or receive signals. Cords plugged into jacks carry video and sound between the VCR and television.

motors (MOH-turs): Motors are parts of a machine that create motion. One of the motors in the VCR causes the drum to spin.

To Learn More

IN THE LIBRARY

Holzweiss, Kristina. *Amazing Makerspace DIY with Electricity*. New York, NY: Scholastic, 2018.

Kenney, Karen Latchana. *Who Invented the Television? Sarnoff vs. Farnsworth*. Minneapolis, MN: Lerner Publishing Group, 2018.

Ringstad, Arnold. *What's Inside a DVD Player?* Mankato, MN: The Child's World, 2020.

ON THE WEB

Visit our website for links about taking apart a VCR: **childsworld.com/links**

Note to Parents, Teachers, and Librarians: We routinely verify our Web links to make sure they are safe and active sites. So encourage your readers to check them out!

Index